T0118317

# The Magic
# of Believing
# Action Plan

**The Master Class Series**

# The Magic of Believing Action Plan

A MASTER CLASS COURSE WITH

## Mitch Horowitz

MEDIA

Published 2020 by Gildan Media LLC
aka G&D Media
www.GandDmedia.com

FIRST EDITION 2020

Cover design by Tom McKeveny

Interior design by Meghan Day Healey of Story Horse, LLC

Library of Congress Cataloging-in-Publication Data is available upon request

ISBN: 978-1-7225-0232-4

10   9   8   7   6   5   4   3   2   1

# Contents

# Preface

I consider *The Magic of Believing* one of the greatest books ever written on harnessing and using the creative and causative powers of your mind. The book has been an enormous influence on my life and search. Over the span of these five lessons, we take a deep dive into the most actionable and powerful ideas in *The Magic of Believing* and also explore advances in science and spiritual insight that have occurred since Claude M. Bristol published the book in 1948, and how they augment his ideas.

*The Magic of Believing* is a book that has improved with age. Its insights and instincts are supported by a wide range of recent findings in placebo studies, psychical research, neuroplasticity, and quantum theory, as we will explore. But Claude did not write as a spiritual visionary or scientist. He wrote as a journalist and businessman who related to the needs of everyday people, and who discovered a personal metaphysics that could be widely shared and applied.

I have spent a large part of my career in spiritual publishing. At one point it occurred to me that a majority of the successful books I published—books that not only succeeded upon their launch but also seemed bound for posterity—were written by people in middle age or beyond. Claude M. Bristol fits this pattern. He did not publish *The Magic of Believing* until he was 57. He died too young, just three years later. The book was written with the pen of his life. It frames ideas that he had practiced for decades and proved in his lived experience.

We are going to examine and expand on Claude's lessons, and whenever more recent methods augment Claude's own, I offer them to you. I believe that by the end of these five sessions you will find deeper, richer, fuller, and more meaningful uses of the ideas in this great book. In the afterword, "Claude M. Bristol and the Metaphysics of Success," I share a 2016 article in which I explore Claude's life and significance. That short piece holds lessons of its own.

Whether you're new to *The Magic of Believing* or if you've read it multiple times, this course will renew your sense of spirit, action, and possibility.

—Mitch Horowitz

# CHAPTER ONE

# Magician
of Believing

It is meaningful for me to begin this first lesson with a look at the man who was Claude M. Bristol (1891–1951). I firmly believe that practical lessons can be drawn from the life of every exceptional person—and especially those who wrote books of practical metaphysics based on their own individual, immediate experience.

It is almost impossible to understand the fullness of the ideas in Claude's book without knowing something about the man himself. Claude M. Bristol was born in Portland, Oregon in 1891. He spent most of his career as a journalist and businessman. Bristol was widely known throughout the west as a crack newspaper and magazine writer. He learned his craft as a police reporter for newspapers in Oregon. Few forms of training do more to sharpen and prepare you for work as a writer, journalist, or researcher than police reporting.

I also began my career as a police reporter, so I can identify with Claude's path. In that atmosphere, you function under tight deadlines in stressful and rarely friendly situations. You learn to gather facts quickly and produce crystal-clear copy. Or you sink. That's where Bristol's chops as a writer came from. He was sufficiently recognized as a journalist so that Palmer Hoyt (1946–1979), the widely respected editor-in-chief of *The Denver Post*, wrote the introduction to the first edition of *The Magic of Believing*, an unusual foray for a newspaper-man into metaphysics.

While still a young man, Bristol experienced an unusual turn in life, which got him on the scent trail of practical metaphysics. You may be able to identify very personally with his story, especially as I am writing these words in the midst of the 2020 coronavirus pandemic and the financial disasters it has wrought.

We frequently approach books of New Thought, mind power, and practical metaphysics because we find ourselves confronted with deep and unexpected needs. We often come to these books seeking financial solutions. Perhaps we are trying to break out of a rut in our career or maybe in our personal life. We come perhaps rebounding from a broken relationship. We come looking for a greater sense of personal power and the ability to see through our wishes in life.

Bristol found himself at just such a crossroads. It was during World War I when he entered the military service in 1918, the final year of that catastrophic conflict. At that time, American forces were fully engaged and Bristol found himself stationed in France. He later went on to write for the Army newspaper *Stars and Stripes*, but early in his career he was a standard grunt hauling around ammunition and supplies in dangerous battlefield conditions. Because of a snafu in his transfer papers, Bristol was receiving no pay. For weeks he was unable to purchase a stick of gum, a cigarette, or candy bar. He experienced an acute sense of longing every time he saw another GI light up a cigarette or throwaway a gum wrapper. He thought, "That is everything I can't do."

He had a place to sleep on the ground. He had meals supplied by the Army. But for a long stretch he was penniless. Bristol vowed that someday he would have lots of money. He would never again find himself in that situation. He swore that when he got out of the Army and returned to the States he would spend the rest of his life in prosperity.

This experience ignited in Claude the one thing that is critical to every mind-power program, and I ask you to take it very seriously. It is having *a passionate, absolute, definite, and unshakable aim.* That is the dividing line between success and failure in any program of self-development whether metaphysical, therapeutic or both.

Your desire must be specific. It is insufficient to have a wishy-washy, half-committed desire or a general wish for things to get better. You must not hedge or be embarrassed about your desire. It belongs to you alone. You don't have to vet it with anybody else. You don't need anybody else's approbation. Claude wished for money, which he writes about very plainly in *The Magic of Believing.*

What is your wish? Remember, you don't have to share it with anybody. In fact, it's better not to. It's better to be silent because you don't want to invite the opinion of someone who's going to break down your mental resolve, who's going to randomly criticize you, or who's going to tell you in so many words that you're not being "spiritual enough." I don't make distinctions in my search between inner and outer, personality and essence, higher and lower, spiritual and material. It's all one thing. It's one life. And it's yours.

You may be possessed by a deeply felt need for which you have very good reasons. That need may be for money. That need may be for something you wish to produce in the world like a work of art or a business innovation. That need may be to excel in your field whether you're a soldier, schoolteacher, or salesperson—whatever it is, you may feel a profound hunger for it. You mustn't feel embarrassed by your need. Do not get melancholy or self-doubtful about it. The driving engine of all progress is the urgency to repair something.

"There's a relationship between pain and excellence." A brilliant filmmaker named Jacqueline Castel told me that. That principle reverberates through Claude's story. He suffered want—and that drove him toward a desire. That desire, in turn, drove him towards practical metaphysics. When he arrived back in the States there were various opportunities awaiting him, both within finance and within journalism. He actually divided his career across both.

Whatever he was doing, he would sit at his desk and on a pad or pieces of scrap paper, whatever was at hand, he would doodle dollar signs, all day long. He did this when he was on the telephone, in meetings, or contemplating ideas. He was absolutely ignited by this idea, this want, this need for money. It never left him. It mushroomed into a career that was not only multi-faceted but also very remunerative. It included a successful writing career.

Claude wrote only two books. The first appeared in 1932. It was a pamphlet-sized work called *TNT: It Rocks the Earth*. *TNT* was a digest of some of his early mind-power philosophy—the idea that what you believe, what you feel, what you think, and your mental pictures will concretize in the world around you. Later in this book, we are going to explore why this is so and how this works. It wasn't until 1948 that Claude published *The Magic of Believing*. He was 57 years old and died just three years later.

I can relate again. I didn't publish my first book *Occult America* until I was past 40. I don't want you to feel daunted by conventional boundaries. Yes, we do experience physical limitations. We experience limitations in geography, income, and various other ways. But I want you to fix in your mind that the man who wrote one of the greatest, most enduring, and widely read books of practical metaphysics of the 20th century did not publish it until he was 57 years old. That's among the reasons the book is solid—because it is written from lived experience.

He also had good training. He had a background as a journalist and, as I mentioned, a police reporter, which is boot camp for any writer. A lot of people tell me—maybe you're one of them—that they want to write. How should they get started? (Wanting to get published is different from wanting to write—don't confuse the two.) I always say to start with the basics of journalism. Learn how to write a lead paragraph. Learn the five W's: who, what, when, where, and why. Learn the basics of old-time wire service writing. Do this and you will have a foundation beneath your feet that will never fail you.

Don't be hasty or fickle. Take the time to hone your craft. That was part of Claude's greatness as a writer. Again, the man only wrote two books in his lifetime. The first, *TNT*, was more of a pamphlet. *The Magic of Believing* was a full-throated and substantial book—and an immediate success. Some celebrities say that Claude's book put them on their path. The comedian Phyllis Diller (1917–2012) was a big fan of *The Magic of Believing*. The brashly funny performer said she suffered from crushing shyness until she had found her way to Claude's book. She recommended it throughout her life and often spoke of it in interviews.

Liberace (1919–1987) was an enormous fan of *The Magic of Believing*. So much so that in

1956, the stage performer recorded an original song in tribute called "The Magic of Believing." There also appeared a "Liberace edition" of *The Magic of Believing*, which featured his image on the cover and for which the artist wrote a special foreword. Arnold Schwarzenegger has spoken glowingly of *The Magic of Believing*. My friend George Noory, the host of Coast to Coast AM, credits the book with setting his career in motion.

Many successful people credit their achievements to Claude's book—and I actually believe that this five-part course could mark a turning point in your life. These lessons and Claude's book could be the very thing you've been waiting for. I don't say that cheaply or with hyperbole. Strange things happen when people discover this program. I can't tell you precisely why, although I'm going to offer you some theories and very strong possibilities.

For now, I want to offer just one remarkable and true story that came to my personal attention. I offer you this story not with a guarantee that it's going to happen to you, and not with the claim that miracles will suddenly come showering into your life, but rather with a simple, basic promise that every word I am about to relate to you is absolutely true as I heard it.

One evening I went on Facebook and posted a picture of my 1948 vintage edition of *The Magic of Believing*. Along with the image, I issued a challenge to my social media followers: "Let's try to approach this book with what in Zen Buddhism is called 'beginner's mind'." I continued: "Let's pretend that it's 1948 and *The Magic of Believing* has just rolled off the presses. We are all holding first editions in our hands. Let's stay up into the night together and read this book." I believe that a spiritual power or a pooling of mental resources arises from group activities. Focused group activities tend to heighten intuition and intellect and refine emotions. So, I put out this challenge to my friends and said, "Sit in a chair with me up late into the night and let's approach these ideas as though for the very first time."

It so happens that when I posted this challenge, it caught the eye of a friend who was living in New England. He was recovering from a severe and longstanding illness. While recuperating, my friend had fallen into a desperate financial crisis. He had been unable to work. He was down to $102 in the bank. He had no health insurance (a national disgrace that I hope is ameliorated for people reading these words in the future), no source of income, and no immediate prospects.

He told himself, "I have nothing to lose. I may as well take up this challenge." He happened to own an audio edition of *The Magic of Believing*, which I had narrated. He played this audio edition over and over. It became his constant companion for about a week. He sometimes listened in marathon sessions. A few days into this he received a call from a former boss.

While they were catching up on things, the ex-boss said, "By the way, you really ought to look at your old 401K." My friend had maintained such an account but not rolled it over when he left this employer. My friend sighed and said, "Oh that—what's the big deal?" He thought there were just a few dollars in it. His ex-boss told him, "No, really. I'm being serious with you. You've got to check your 401K." The ex-boss said that more than $50,000 was sitting dormant in his account. My friend had no idea that he had accumulated such a sum of money.

He was recovering from a very severe illness so his eye wasn't necessarily on finances as it might have been at another time in life. He had no idea there was $50,000 with his name on it. This call arrived a few days into his marathon listen of *The Magic of Believing*. Was it coincidence? Perhaps. Was he wishfully projecting a pattern onto something? Could be. Was it a miracle? Well, the news reached him in a fashion that emotionally felt miraculous.

I am not suggesting that this course or *The Magic of Believing* is going to produce some miracle in your life. But let me offer you a possibility, and this is certainly something that Claude believed himself and that we're going to explore in greater depth.

I believe very strongly that there are extra-physical dimensions to thought. As I describe in the next chapter, there exists too much evidence to write off that possibility. In fact, we have so much evidence of there being some extra-physical, non-local capacity to the mind—much of this evidence derived from rigorous laboratory experiments across fields including medicine, physics, and academically-backed psychical research—that materialist philosophy doesn't cover all the bases of life. It simply no longer works in the 21st century.

The idea that matter alone creates itself and that your mind is just a byproduct of the physical organ of your brain doesn't hold up. We possess too much data from placebo studies, neuroplasticity, psi research, and various branches of quantum theory to allow for the mind as a strictly local phenomenon. In short, it's possible that what you're routinely thinking about is transmitting itself, so to speak, to other beings in ways that we do not yet fully understand.

When your mind is profoundly and deeply focused on something, you may be constantly sending out a kind of communication, a kind of signal to other people who may be able to help you, who may be able to meet you halfway. Claude goes further with that question. He reasons that the mind possesses vibrational or frequency-like signals that can result not only telepathy but in telekinesis or the preferred term psychokinesis.

I regard some of his language as metaphorical because we're always dealing in imagery when we're just on the cusp of understanding something that we haven't fully grasped. But I must also add that Claude's supposition is not as far off as it may sound. The scientist J.B. Rhine conducted psychokinesis experiments for several years at Duke University. Under rigorously controlled laboratory conditions he found that certain subjects were capable of affecting throws of dice. Later psychical experimenters at Princeton University found that certain subjects were able to affect the pattern of numbers appearing on a device called a random number generator, which emits infinite combinations of random numerals. Through intention they created instances of symmetry where there was none. Although I am describing these experiments in brief, they have been subject to greater scrutiny than most trials used to test for the effectiveness of popular pharmaceuticals.

I also believe Claude's instinct was correct that what you think about is communicated, at least intermittently, in some extra-physical manner. That's one reason why when you are fixated on a solution, and you're thinking about it constantly and productively, you may be sending out a communiqué to others who have something to offer you, who might be able to lend assistance or suggestion. Perhaps this occurred for my friend when his ex-boss reached out to him at the most desperate moment of his life, at a moment of absolute financial despair, to share news of a bank account with $50,000 that belonged to him.

Skeptics insist that our brains are designed to impose patterns on things. That is true. But skeptics rarely apply this logic to themselves. Their first impulse is almost always to rationalize anomalies. That is understandable and even healthy. But events like the one I just described are difficult to quantify. This is due to the complexity of emotions involved. Seen from one perspective, a remarkable web of events exists at the back of virtually *everything* that happens to you, whether seemingly exceptional or mundane. But factors of emotional impact, timing, and profundity of need are highly individualized, making anomalous experiences difficult to quantify, reify, or measure. Not everything in life can be broken down on an actuarial table.

I've noted the importance of knowing what you truly want in life—of having a definite, absolute aim. I want you to write down that aim, not on a handheld device, not on a tablet or laptop, but in a tactile way with a pen or pencil and paper.

I believe that when you write down a wish, the very act of committing in a physical manner is the first step of actualization. Think of it: when you write something down on paper, you not only have a vow and contract, you not only have clarified and committed, but you have, in however nascent a fashion, altered reality. The writing on that paper has created something palpably real that was not there before.

It's a first step, however small, toward the production of what you wish to see in the world. Always take first steps seriously. Claude would spend his workdays doodling, writing dollar signs on a little pad of paper. He was constantly reinforcing what he wanted. Think carefully about what you want, because it's very powerful. Be sure that you are being honest with yourself. Be sure that you are not curbed by some sense of embarrassment, shame, or internalized peer pressure.

We all want to look good in the eyes of others. We want to be appreciated and admired.

We all have some handed-down ideas of how to achieve that. I invite you as an experiment to dispense with all that. Go out for a walk or sit in meditation or lie down and give yourself permission to really ponder what you want in life; hold it up for no one else's approval; be silent about it; seek not even your own approval.

One of the mental traps that limits your creativity and sense of self is the habit of rote thought. We tell ourselves things over the course of our lives that seem so familiar that we do not question them. A spiritual person might think: "I don't want money. I want inner awareness." There is nothing wrong with that and I'm not putting that down. But you must be sure it is true. Do not use such statements to obfuscate what you really want.

A corporate go-getter might say, "I want to advance up the ranks. I want to run things." But he or she might actually harbor an unacknowledged wish to stay at home, to nest, to be private. Again, there's nothing wrong with that if it's sincere. Truth liberates.

When I advise being silent about your aim, I mean not only avoiding random talk, but also affording yourself the liberty of not even consulting the habitual, repeat voices or standards that you've set up in your head.

I talked about approaching *The Magic of Believing* with beginner's mind. That's very powerful. You can practice this with regard to your aim, as well. Ask yourself, "What do I really want in life?" without reference to anything that's come before.

My only condition is that your goal be *actionable*—that there is some way, however small, that you can begin acting on it. A goal that is not actionable is escapism or a daydream.

Let the first, smallest step be writing down your goal. Be sure about it. Spend however long a period you need on this. That's one of the wonderful things about this Master Class. You go at your own pace. You don't have to return until you've really formulated it; or if you wish to proceed before you've fully formulated it, that's fine too. The only rule is: *begin*.

# CHAPTER TWO

# Why Thoughts Make Things Happen

This lesson deals with the *how* and the *why* of mind metaphysics. Why does any of this material work? Is there really a "magic of believing" and what does science say about it?

If anything, insights that have emerged in the past century from quantum physics, psychical research, neuroplasticity, placebo studies and other fields have reaffirmed Claude M. Bristol's central thesis, which is that *thoughts make things happen*; that belief has a power that exceeds cognition or motor skills.

Something is set into motion when you harbor a deeply held belief. But why should anything be happening at all? Is it just our imagination? And what is imagination?—this mysterious force that can cause people to experience physical wellness simply because they experience hopeful expectancy, such as when given a placebo pill. What is this *imagination* that seems to bring people together at the most propitious moments? What is this power of belief that seems to develop a person's life, as my life has developed, according to his or her inner pictures and emotionalized thoughts?

I want to talk about the *how* and *why* of mind metaphysics, because I believe it's important to approach this topic with clarity and plain language. I don't lean on phrases like "manifesting" or "law of attraction." I have no intractable problem with those terms, but they do not explain enough. Using them is somewhat like writers in the 19th century routinely using the term "soul." We must be more concrete. Otherwise we do not grow beyond familiar platitudes and ideas. What is the soul? What is the imagination? What is the mind? Why should there be any congruity between thought and event?

In short: what is the "magic of believing," and how does it work?

I want to start by exploring ways in which the power of thought can appear in your life.

I'm going to discuss a wide range of issues that are not always directly found in Claude's work—some of these advances came to light after his death—but are closely related to his ideas. I think he would have felt deeply validated by what we are now going to explore.

I believe that two stages occur when you hold an idea that you wish to see actualized in the world. The first is *gestation*, the period of time from when you think of something to when it starts to unfold. The second is *channels of delivery*, which is the emergence of active means by which the event, thing, or condition reaches you. After I review these ideas, I consider the question of *why* anything seems to be happening at all when you release a focused thought.

First, we'll consider gestation or the passage of time. When you hold fast to a thought—and I hope you're underway in devising your definite aim—you experience a *time interval* between your deeply held wish and its concretization. The gestation period could occur quickly, or it could require months or even years. The latter was the case in my life.

Let me share a personal experience, because I feel that as a co-seeker I should be self-disclosing. For many years I worked in book publishing. I was an editor and executive at large New York publishing companies, where

I worked for nearly three decades. I was never fully satisfied with it.

I worked with great commitment, always dedicated to my writers and books, and I had some notable successes. Yet it all felt secondary. Publishing felt to me like a glorified day job. But I didn't know what my passion really was. It wasn't until years into my publishing career that I finally rediscovered myself as a writer and speaker—and I realized that my passion was to document metaphysical experience in history and practice.

This is why I write today as both a historian and as a practical seeker. In each case I am seeking empiricism, historically and personally. The only real empiricism on the practical spiritual path is experience and conduct. What else could practical philosophy mean? At the same time, we benefit immeasurably from understanding the *background* of the ideas we work with. Historical understanding serves to enrich your search. The more fully you understand your thought lineage, the more you can discover linkages and new possibilities. Hence, I call myself a believing historian.

But for years of my adult life I was not writing, speaking, or presenting, other than at sales conferences. As a result, I often felt like I stood for nothing. As I entered into my fullness as a writer, however, a new sense of purpose opened to me. The new purpose was accompanied by a wide range of opportunities, including work in screen, television, movies, and audio narrations.

I am writing these words at age 54. And I must tell you that the work I am doing today is the mind's eye image of some of the earliest dreams, visions, and wishes that I harbored as a child, even as young as four or five.

Even from that early age I recall deeply wanting to be in front of the camera, microphone, and writing pad, whether it took the form of a typewriter, as it might have in my mind back then, or a tablet or a computer as it would today. When I played games with neighborhood friends in Queens, whether it was some version of cops and robbers or cowboys and Indians, or whatever—the kinds of things kids engage in as fantasy play—I was experiencing my own internal drama, as I'm sure my friends were, too. While I was playing these games, although I was overtly involved, interactive, and committed to the play that was going on, I was imagining being in front of a movie camera, being on a movie set, and I was playing the part of a cop or robber or soldier like an actor. My playmates were undoubtedly imagining their own things. I did not know their internal world, nor they mine.

That seed of desire didn't revisit me in outer experience until midlife. I wanted to present in front of a camera. That's exactly what I'm doing today. I wanted to write. That produced the words you're reading now. I wanted to speak in front of a microphone. Those of you who are listening to this as an audio book can warrant the result. But I must emphasize that I did not see results for years—and just because you may not see results immediately or even for years does not mean that those results are not developing, gestating, and coming toward you.

A popular expression runs through our culture: "Be careful what you wish for, you just might get it." I asked myself one day where did that expression come from. And is it true? I felt skeptical toward this principle because whatever you wish for, whatever you want to move toward, is always gong to carry some consequence, intended or not. Everything in life, including doing nothing, carries unexpected consequence.

Sometimes I think we get hung up on the question of consequence. A person might worry that if he asks for money it could reach him in some tragic way. Another person might worry that if he asks for a new job it might come through some violent upheaval. Although I urge you to frame your desires ethically—by which I mean with a sense of reciprocity toward others—I also ask you to remember that there are *always* unintended consequences, whether you're passive or active. There is always some unforeseen concession.

So, I am not overly troubled by the expression, "Be careful what you wish for, you just might get it." At the same time the principle does convey something valuable. Hence, I wanted to learn its origin. When we go to the source, we often discover different folds of meaning within seemingly familiar ideas. This is among the reasons why I combine historicism with spiritual search.

In short, I learned that the expression was popularized by Ralph Waldo Emerson, the great Transcendentalist writer who produced extraordinary essays and lectures from the mid-to-late 1800s. Emerson, in turn, was gleaning the principle from the philosopher Goethe (1749–1832). Taking a leaf from Goethe's *Faust,* Emerson wrote in his 1860 essay "Fate":

> And the moral is that what we seek we shall find; what we flee from flees from us; as Goethe said, "what we wish for in youth, comes in heaps on us in old age," too often cursed with the granting of our prayer: and hence the high caution, that, since we are sure of having what we wish, we must beware to ask only for high things.

\* \* \*

Some might object to that reasoning. Some of us complain of having all kinds of unrealized dreams, high or low. But take a pause. What have you truly gone through life thinking about? Sometimes we falsely believe that we've wished for high things, or that our wishes have formed coherence and purpose. Yet our minds and emotions are rarely focused, and are often riddled with distractions and conflicting aims.

This is why I keep emphasizing the need for a definite wish. Life eventually bends to thought and, baring some overwhelmingly countervailing measure such as a health crisis, you will get some variant of what you wish for. I contend that if you examine your life as it exists today and your internal life as it existed from the dawn of your earliest memories, you will discover an uncanny congruency. Try it.

I was shocked to realize that things I had been thinking about when I was very young, which I've disclosed to you, have manifested, albeit in a somewhat different form. Making that discovery was like awakening to a whole different dimension of my character.

I just talked about interval and gestation. Now I want to consider the *channels* or means of arrival. My dream reached me, but in a way that I was not necessarily able to foresee. It came to me through available channels. This is very important, because when your wish reaches you, it is likely to arrive through *established means.*

It is unlikely that the world is going to remake itself to accommodate you. If you want money, for example, you are probably not going to find a stack of bills sitting on your coffee table one night. You will not find a proverbial pot of gold in the kitchen when you get up to make coffee. The greater likelihood is that what is sought will reach you through an established channel that is plain and actual, but that you may have overlooked. That's why I often counsel people to be intently watchful when working with the power of belief.

Your wish may arrive through channels that seem routine or ordinary, so much so that you're apt to overlook them, like my friend in New England who didn't think to look back at his 401K, who had to be persuaded to look someplace where a large sum of money was waiting for him. It was an established channel. But it was neglected.

Also be on the lookout for things to reach you in a highly unusual way, one that is outside your sense of possibilities. That also happened to me. As I was working on my first book *Occult America*, which appeared in 2009, I found that even a couple of years leading up to publication, as word of my research got out, I started receiving television offers from The History Channel, The Montel Williams Show, and other cable networks and shows.

When my book came out, I appeared on Dateline NBC, CBS Sunday Morning, NPR's All Things Considered, CNN—I appeared in a wide range of places. I wasn't an actor playing a part but there I was in front of the camera, the place that I dreamed of as a very little kid. You must not overlook outlying alternatives and possibilities regarding channels of delivery.

Maybe you're ill and you're looking for recovery. The means could arrive in the form of a pill (never discount conventional options). They could also come through some alternative modality, such as a friend inviting you to an energy medicine seminar or something of that nature. Life is a polarity: don't overlook obvious channels and don't overlook unusual channels. *Eschewing prejudice* is the best way to avoid missing the needed thing or condition.

Not only must you watch carefully, but also say yes to promising things when they reach you. The philosopher Jacob Needleman once asked me, "What do you do when someone offers you a gift?" I stared blankly at him. "You accept it," he said. You accept it. It sounds simple. But it is easy to overlook things that reach us through the magic of believing.

When you're being offered a gift—as I believe you will be—do not slice and dice and tear it apart. Do not doubt or ignore it either because it seems too routine or it doesn't fit your mind's eye picture. Accept it.

Assuming I am correct about the power of thought, *why should anything be happening at all?* One of the things I treasure about Claude M. Bristol is that he was among the few popular metaphysical writers of his era (and ours) who was well versed in ESP research, a field that is very important to me.

In *The Magic of Believing*, Claude writes about my personal hero, J.B. Rhine the pioneering psychical researcher who worked for years at Duke University starting in the early 1930s. J.B. was famous for card experiments to test for ESP. In clinical trials, J.B. used a deck of cards with five suits or images called Zener cards from which he asked subjects to select which card he had picked. Out of five suits the subject had a 20 percent chance of guessing correctly. But across tens of thousands of trials some subjects cumulatively and continually scored beyond the 20 percent guess rate. It might not be dramatically higher—it might be 28 percent, it might be 35 percent, it might be slightly upwards of there—but it was a detectible, continual spike across thousands of trials. The results broke the law of averages. They couldn't be explained.

Through heavily juried and scrutinized experimentation, J.B. and his colleagues determined beyond statistical doubt that there exists anomalous transfer of information in a laboratory setting. This data transfer occurs outside of ordinary sensory experience. He called it Extra-Sensory Perception or ESP.

J.B. also studied the effect of thought on dice rolls, or psychokinesis, and he continually found, in rigorous and controlled conditions, which were subject to the most withering scrutiny and analysis of critics—both honest critics and polemical critics—that the mind evinces some measure of extra-physicality. His data has never been explained or overturned.

Despite whatever people may read, which is usually whatever comes up as the first five search results on Google, or whatever may appear in Wikipedia—which is unfortunately a poor source for this material—J.B.'s data has stood up. He demonstrated as closely as we can with clinical certainty that our thoughts evince causation beyond the five senses.

In the previous lesson, I ventured how thoughts may somehow broadcast themselves, so to speak. This may be going on constantly or intermittently depending on one's emotional state. Another of J.B.'s findings, which he relegated to a footnote but which I found extraordinary, is that an atmosphere of *hopeful expectancy* among experimenters and subjects seemed to correlate with spikes in results. If the subject was in a buoyant mood, and was feeling positively predisposed towards the experiment, results would rise. If the subject was bored, restless, or tired, results dipped. Then, if the subject took a break, had a conversation, had a cup of coffee, whatever it may be, and his or her spirits lifted, so would the results.

As in placebo studies, hopeful expectancy seems to be the catalyst in ESP studies, at least among subjects who demonstrate results. We'll talk about ways to cultivate hopeful expectancy because it does not always come naturally. If it comes naturally to you, consider yourself fortunate. It does not for me.

I first started to experiment with New Thought and mind metaphysics because I am not naturally optimistic. I am not innately possessed of a hopeful outlook. I've never suffered from depression—my particular problem is anxiety. Anxiety can be a friend because it helps you prepare for difficult circumstances. Wariness can save the day; but wariness does not facilitate hopeful expectancy, which seems to be the royal road to results in placebo studies, psychical research, and, I would venture, mind metaphysics. Hence, I had to look for ways to consciously cultivate hopeful expectancy and to control some of the difficult drifts and byways of my thoughts. In later chapters I share some of the methods I've grown to trust.

I mentioned earlier that Claude hypothesized that the mind emits frequencies or vibrations. As noted, those terms could be seen as metaphorical. We sometimes use language as a placeholder when we do not have a theory of delivery.

I want to posit such a theory of delivery. I think it's important to at least try to assay what might be happening. Otherwise we rely on familiar concepts and language, and the search gets reduced to catechism. In that vein, I want look more closely at quantum mechanics, a field that was still in relative infancy when Claude wrote *The Magic of Believing*.

Decades of quantum experiments reveal that subatomic particles exist in an infinite number of positions at once. Researchers sometimes call this a "wave state." Only when a sentient observer makes the decision to take a measurement does a wave collapse, so to speak, and a particle is localized to one definite place. We know that a subatomic particle occupies an infinite number of places, or what is sometimes called "superposition," because researchers detect interference patterns. But only when someone actually takes a measurement does that particle appear in a single place.

There exist many experiments, some of them literal, some of them thought experiments—the most famous of which is called Schrodinger's Cat—which demonstrate that if a particle exists in an infinite number of places at once, *it follows that infinite outcomes are not only possible, but are actually occurring all the time.* The outcome that we individually experience occurs only when an observer takes a measurement.

And how different are our natural senses from the instruments in a particle lab? Aren't our senses organic technologies used to take measurements? We smell, hear, see, touch, and taste. Attention, perspective, and assumption are all acts of measurement.

Why not use this power of measurement to *select*?

Select is my preferred term. As noted, I seldom say "manifest" or "attract." I use select because it's what I believe we are doing all the time, not only in special cases but always as part of our navigation of life. An infinitude of possibilities play out in life, just as in the particle lab; but we do not see this infinitude. This is because we possess coarse instruments of measurement, which are our physical senses. We do not possess finely tuned instruments of observation, hence we experience a kind of "information leakage." We do not see the infinite. But we are nonetheless always selecting among its possibilities.

William Blake wrote: "If the doors of perception were cleansed every thing would appear to man as it is, Infinite." This is why the great metaphysician Neville Goddard, who I have tattooed on my left arm, made the statement: "An assumption, though false, if persisted in will harden into fact." Our minds are part of infinity. They are infinity. They can neither be added to nor subtracted from. In 1948, the same year that Claude published *The Magic of Believing,* Neville stated: "Scientists will one day explain why there is a serial universe. But in practice, how you use this serial universe to change the future is more important."

If life is infinite, then linear time itself must be an illusion. Linearity, as we imagine it—past, present, future—is a very useful, necessary device because it helps us organize life. It is a profoundly necessary illusion. But, as Blake alluded, as quantum theorists have alluded, and as Neville alluded, reality is infinite, shapeless, and timeless; it is a wave state. Everything is possible at once but nothing is experienced without an observer. Hence, when you practice the magic of believing—picturing a desired outcome, holding fast to an ideal, abiding by a cherished assumption, or the opposite of all these things—you are *selecting* events, and thus selecting the past, present, and future.

We sometimes fantasize about going backwards in time and delivering some urgently needed advice to a younger self. Isn't it possible that schema is actually real—and is occurring always? Just as a change in arrangement necessitates other changes, your experience of self, both past and present, alters with your perspective. Reality is ever shifting in infinite directions, including what we call past and future. Yet the results feel entirely linear and orderly. You are at this moment engaged in *infinite selection*. The events that reach your awareness strike you as routine and contextual. But actually your life is forever in flux like a wave state, which bends and localizes based on perception. That is why Emerson cautioned: "'what we wish for in youth, comes in heaps on us in old age,' . . . since we are sure of having what we wish, we must beware to ask only for high things."

Let me recap what we've covered in this lesson. There is a *how* and a *why* to the magic of believing. The *how* is that when we consistently hold an ideal, mental picture, or assumption—either lovely or distressing—it revisits us at unexpected moments. Something may seem to occur quickly, as it did for my friend in New England when he was desperate for money; but something can also unfold over a long stretch of time, as it did for me, and as it may be for you right now.

Consider that there are different kinds of unfoldment, different methods and manners of gestation. Be vigilant. Be a watcher at the gate, because the thoughts that you admit, dwell upon, and emphasize are, I believe, working and creating causes and events in your *life right now.*

Keep in mind that results are likely to arrive through established channels. Watch very carefully for things coming to you. Do not overlook them. Again, be a good watcher at the gate. Do not discard something because it seems routine or comes in a wrapping that differs from what you might have pictured.

And, finally, *why* should anything be happening at all? I contend that we have seen so many developments in psychical research, quantum theory, neuroplasticity, placebo studies, among other fields, that we cannot ignore, turn or walk away from the question of the mind possessing extra-physical abilities.

Likewise, we know enough today to understand that time is not an orderly phenomenon that travels along a single track. Generations ago Einstein demonstrated the relativity of time. Time is not fixed. If you're on earth and a friend of yours is moving at or near light speed in a spaceship, time literally slows down for him. This is demonstrable. This alone tells us time is not what we think it is.

Moreover, data from quantum physics reveals that seemingly fixed objects are also not as they appear. Objects are actualized through perspective. If this is lawfully observed on the subatomic scale it presents implications throughout life—and suggests the infinite and flexible potential of thought. Consider the wonderful possibilities this opens to you. Let us approach *The Magic of Believing* with a great sense of hopeful expectancy. This expectancy is justified and warranted. It is the turnkey that will open you to the extraordinary.

# CHAPTER THREE

# The Power of Personal Style

I now want to explore the power of style and self-image. In some regards, this is a very unusual lesson in terms of our spiritual culture because I'm going to talk about the value of your *outer appearance*—how you dress, your tone of voice, your personal gait and composure, the style you adopt, and the self-image you present.

I say this is unusual, because within much of our spiritual culture we are asked to embrace certain principles as self-evidently true, specifically principles of non-attachment and non-identification. We typically hear that what matters is what we cannot see, and that outer life is ultimately illusion or *samsara*, which the seeker should learn to regard as less and less significant as he or she advances.

I don't think that general principle gets at the real story of our lives. I don't think it encompasses the nature of our existence. In some respects, the ideal of non-attachment is like a carrot forever dangled in front of the seeker; we feel like we're running towards it without getting any closer. I believe the principle of non-attachment to the outer places an unnatural demand on the seeker.

We must be wary of uncritically importing or cherry picking concepts that belong to ancient religious traditions, both Eastern and Western. We encounter certain concepts, often in translations of translations of ancient literature, which we are taught to regard as sacrosanct and inerrant. But actually many religious concepts must be understood and evaluated from the context in which they initially arose.

All religions are the product of human hands. Religions are human attempts to codify and structure our relations with the ineffable. Every religion emerges from its own locality and time period, reflecting civic, legal, and social needs of a particular population. All the great religions offer universally applicable lessons; but all religions also bear traits and markings of the cultures, prejudices, attitudes, and circumstances from which they arose. Hence, I feel strongly that religious precepts must be verified. Otherwise, you are imbibing habit as much as tradition.

Hinduism, or the Vedic faith, is a magnificent, world-changing faith. Likewise, is Buddhism, which sprang from it. I drop to my knees before these traditions. At the same time, these faiths, from which we receive many of our modern ideas about non-identification and non-attachment, grew from times and places where individuals were almost certain to live and die within the social caste they were born into. The human situation was not entirely different within Hebraic and Christian variants of religion in the Mediterranean basin. Sometimes our ancient religions were structured to give solace to people who, within in a given cultural and social order, experienced very little prospect of escaping the gravity of caste, rank, class, tribe, or gender.

For many ancient people, and especially so in caste-based societies, the need to find a sense of self-worth was relegated almost exclusively to a scale of extra-physical values, and of de-emphasizing attachment to worldly goods or rank. This weighed upon the shaping of some of the ancient faiths. These same urgencies do not necessarily comport with how we live today. Nor are they, I believe, absolutes of human nature. I believe that the highest role of men and women is to be generative: to be co-creators within our sphere of existence, in matters both visible and unseen.

I believe that *all* self-expression is sacred. Scripture tells us that God created the individual in his own image. This principle is at the heart of the Greek-Egyptian philosophy called Hermeticism: "As above, so below." If one takes that concept seriously, then it stands to reason that we are intended to self-create, at least within the parameters of our sphere and circumstances. Creativity and self-expression are sacred.

I believe that part of our self-expression, part of the fulfillment of our purpose, part of what helps facilitate our potentials in the world, involves self-image, in all respects and not limited to one definition or another.

I believe there exists complete and total interplay between the inner and the outer. At this point in my search, I do not think of separations between inner and outer, higher and lower, essence and personality, attachment and non-attachment, identification and non-identification, spiritual and material. It's all one thing. "As above, so below."

Contrary to much teaching within alternative spiritual culture, I don't think we are called to downplay, disregard, or deemphasize the so-called exterior as we pursue a fuller sense of life. I think that is artifice. In actuality, attainment of greater selfhood, including in the overt sense, facilitates your ideals, actions, sense of possibility, and the manner in which you relate to others.

In his first book, *TNT,* Claude holds forth brilliantly on the question of artists, businesspeople, and leaders in world affairs conveying a very definite, purposeful, intentional image to their audience, listeners, and constituents.

Claude uses Mahatma Gandhi as an example. He observed that Gandhi, who at that time was fomenting peaceful revolution in what is today the largest democracy in the world, was known for non-violent political change and universal polity. Bristol said that it's not at all cynical to point out that, in addition to Gandhi's political, diplomatic, and ethical genius, he also cultivated a definite image. His walking stick, sandals, spectacles, cropped hair, and traditional robe came from the so-called lower rungs of the caste system in India. His adoption of that appearance is part of what made him into a colossus on the world stage. Claude observes that it can be enormously helpful to the striving individual to cultivate a sense of showmanship. He didn't mean that in a degraded or cynical way. As the newspaper-man he was, he could be blunt and direct.

For those of us who struggle with issues of self-image, as I once did, it can seem very distant to be told to "believe in yourself," be confident, throw back your shoulders and stick out your chest and go through life with a sense of self-possession. There are, of course, affirmations, self-suggestions, and visualizations that can improve self-image from a mental and emotional perspective. We are going to explore some of that material, which I deeply honor and value. In addition to affirmations, however, there are physical steps that heighten self-image and make you a more persuasive and formidable person in the world.

In certain regards, though not all, appearance is an innate trait. We all have things that we like about our appearance and gait, and other things about which we're insecure. These are complexities that every individual must deal with, and some are culturally conditioned. But even within those parameters, you possess greater freedom and possibilities than you may think for a revolution in outer self-image that speaks to your wishes.

I see life as one whole, just as humanity is one whole. We live within a framework of cosmic reciprocity or what is sometimes called karma. I believe the same is true of your personhood. We are made to feel that we're in pieces; but the interplay of so-called inner and outer is so intimate and total that I believe we misunderstand human nature when we refer to those things separately.

In that vein, let me ask you a question. Are you dressing as you wish? When you get up in the morning, whether it's a weekday, work-day, weekend, vacation, or whatever, are you comporting yourself in such a way that feels natural? How *exactly* do you want to dress in the world? How do you want to wear your hair? How do you want to wear your makeup? What image, what persona, do you feel most comfortable projecting? Don't get lost in thinking that I am just talking about the outer shell of things. Again, I believe in no difference, finally, between the kernel and the shell. It's one great interplay. You are given the gift as a co-creator of crafting your image, and it will reverberate through your entire being.

Again, I ask: How do you want to dress in the world? How do you want to comport your-self? What gait do you want to walk with? How do you want to wear your hair? Do you want to wear bodily adornments like jewelry, tattoos or other things? Even if present circumstances make it impossible for you to dress and com-pose yourself how you wish, you should still know *what that way is*. Live from that mental picture. The day will come, perhaps sooner than you think, where you will actually be able to act on it. But that day won't arrive unless you really ask yourself the question.

What I am describing does not have to do exclusively with physical presentation. It has to do with other cues and signals, such as tone of voice. When I was very young, I served an internship at a newspaper in upstate New York. I knew a police reporter who was very effective and talented, and capable of cultivating good relations with the cops and finding his way in and out of the folds of different stories. He was a man of slight build, very slender, and rather short. In conventional terms, he might seem to cut a rather slight figure. But when he opened his mouth to speak, out came this beautiful, rich, sonorous voice—a very deep bass voice and it got people to listen. It colored his character. I never knew whether it was natural or affect but it completely changed his relations with the world.

On many occasions I have observed striking and charismatic people who, if they possessed some lesser degree of personal style, might have been considered rather unremarkable, at least on first impression. But through their ability to cultivate a definite style, look, or to create something memorable—the frames of their glasses, how they wear a hat, their manner of dress—the self-image that they cultivated made them magnetic. And it did more than that. It made them feel self-possessed and better able to approach people for what they wanted.

The 2012 science-fiction movie *Prometheus* offers an interesting insight in this regard. One of its characters is an android named David, who turns out to be a rather malevolent figure, but who also has his own point of view on creation and reality. In an arresting scene, David, who has been created by man but seeks to surpass his creators, is shown fashioning his self-image while watching the classic movie *Lawrence of Arabia*. David combs his hair in the style of the character of Lawrence. He speaks with the clipped accent of the figure of Lawrence, reciting his lines as if programing himself. I watched this thinking, don't each of us do this all the time, albeit unconsciously?

We populate our perceptions with images, parables, and ideals that we wish to cultivate within. Of course, we live in a very consumer-driven, often conformist, and very media-saturated environment. But what I am describing has been true from time immemorial. Every culture from the Mayans to the Polynesians, from the Hebraic to the Hellenic, had its ideals of beauty and adornment. There is nothing new in the human situation.

If a certain image or idea attracts you, allow yourself to experiment with it. What you discover may be the exact opposite of conformity: you may find that you're engaged in an act of self-selection and self-creation, which, as with the figure of David in *Prometheus*, allows you to surpass the boundaries set around your functioning.

Why not give one day to showing up somewhere comported and dressed in exactly the way you want. See what happens. See what kind of impact or influence it has on you and the people around you. There may be people around you who don't like it or who run you down. Maybe those are the very people to get away from. Maybe those relationships have been long overdue for reconsideration. Why should you be in proximity to people who aren't responsive to your self-image?

At one time in my life I started getting tattoos, which I thoroughly enjoy having. A good friend said with the best of intentions: "Hey, I'm a little worried about you getting all these tattoos because it might serve to close off opportunities to you." I responded, without conceit: "I hear what you're saying, but just watch the offers roll in." They did roll in. I share this to underscore that *more doors opened when I gravitated toward an appearance I found self-expressive.* Rather than get worried that an off-center look would limit my possibilities, my instinct was the opposite.

An artist friend once told me: "Anyone who wants to be a public persona should be able to be reproduced as an action figure—and be immediately recognizable." There's great truth to that. The characters that we venerate—celebrities, sports figures, authors—are easily identified. They bear very recognizable traits. This is true of our archetypes, including in mythology: Mercury holds a caduceus or wand with serpents wrapped around it; Pan holds a lyre or harp; Hercules, a club; Dianna, a bow and arrow of the hunt. What are your personal symbols?

Many people we admire cultivate a self-image. Later in life, Steve Jobs embraced the idea of wearing a daily uniform. He had visited a Japanese factory and was very taken with the crisp, clean, and identifiable uniforms that employees wore. He decided to fashion a uniform for himself. He wanted his selection not only to convey an image of independence but also to be comfortable and convenient, dispensing with fuss. The adoption of a uniform meant one less thing to think about as he started his day. Jobs had a designer produce several hundred units of an identical black turtleneck. He bought New Balance sneakers and Levi's jeans in commensurate numbers.

He wore this ensemble every day for years. It became a personal insignia.

Barack Obama had a similar practice. He said he always wore a blue-gray suit, not only because it looked presidential, but also because it eliminated superfluous decision-making. Mark Zuckerberg wears t-shirts and hoodies. It makes him look like a relaxed Northern California startup dude rather than a tech titan.

You can fashion a uniform, too, so that everyday you look your best, you are at ease and relaxed, you project the image you want, and you can dress each day and pack for travel with minimum fuss. For me it is t-shirts, leather boots, black jeans, and leather jackets. It's who I am. It's easy. It's versatile.

When you make that selection it will go to the core of your being, not because it's influencing from the outside in, but because it's already part of the core.

Let me conclude with an inner truth of life. Other people are always approaching you for what they do not have. They're always looking to others for what they need, for what they feel is deficient in their lives. You do yourself no favors by seeking to accommodate other people, because they're not coming to you for what they already possess. Rather they're seeking to compensate their perceived deficits. If you present yourself as an iconic or self-directed persona you not only become more appealing, but your self-crafted image, as you hone it, eventually reflects who you really are. It is not a mask. It is the shedding of a mask.

# CHAPTER FOUR

# Reconditioning Self-Image

Many of us look out at the world and feel threatened, anxious, or depressed. Some of these thought patterns extend back to our earliest years. These patterns are not strictly matters of conditioning, but conditioning reinforces them. Some of our most deep-seated emotions and thoughts possess an innate quality, which we call temperament or character.

In my observation, we enter the world with a very definite temperament. I remember the indelible impression that both of my sons entered the world with a pronounced character, which I saw evidenced in earliest infancy and which is evident in their adolescence selves today

Temperament is mysterious. It colors how you view other people and how you view your surrounding environment; whether you accommodate or resist others, whether you feel that others are going to do the same to you. These earliest attributes of temperament set in motion a cycle of habitual thoughts, which develop in tandem with our environment. This is what we consider conditioning. Hence, we are all a mixture of temperament and environment, and most psychologists consider these patterns firmly fixed around age 12.

I invite you to think back for a few moments to your earliest childhood memories; back to a time when you just began to retain conscious memories, perhaps around age three. How did you regard yourself? What were your likes, dislikes, fears, and perceived strengths? How did you relate to your siblings? How did you relate to other kids you might have come into contact with in playgroups? How did you regard strangers? Were they objects of interest and fascination? Or were they figures around whom you felt that you needed to be wary? How did you relate to your parents? How did you relate to yourself? Did you feel yourself capable or afraid and needing to run and hide?

Give yourself an opportunity now and after this lesson to really think back to your earliest, most primal memories. Chances are you will discover the template to your personality and to how you go through life today. Those earliest memories are a precious and delicate mix of temperament and environment. They are the basic fiber of existence that got refined through repetition and feelings of security or danger.

Our goal as self-created beings, and probably a great deal of why you approach a book like *The Magic of Believing* or a lesson plan like this one, is to recondition yourself. The primary tool we possess for reconditioning, and one that Claude Bristol dwells upon a great deal in *The Magic of Believing*, is self-suggestion or autosuggestion.

To a great extent, self-suggestion entered modern life in the mid-to-late 19th century through the so-called Nancy School of hypnotism in France. The Nancy hypnotists believed that hypnotism possessed therapeutic potentials. Nancy theorists believed that by placing an individual into a trance state, where the mind is very supple and flexible, and the logical defenses are down, the hypnotist could introduce new ideas of prowess and wellness. Nancy hypnotists sought to relieve self-imposed lim-

itations, psychosomatic illnesses, and irratio-
nal fears.

One of the greatest of the Nancy hypnotists
is a figure about whom I speak and write often,
Emile Coué. Born in Brittany in 1857, Emile
Coué developed an early interest in hypnotism,
which he pursued through a mail-order course
from Rochester, New York. Coué studied hypnotic methods more rigorously in the late 1880s
with one of the founders of the Nancy School.
While working in the early 1900s as a pharma-
cist in Troyes, in northwestern France, Coué
made a startling discovery: Patients responded
better to medications when he spoke in praise
of the formula. Coué came to believe that the
imagination aided not only recovery but also a
person's general sense of wellbeing. From this
insight, Coué developed his method of "conscious autosuggestion." This was essentially a
form of waking hypnosis that involved repeat-
ing confidence-building mantras in a relaxed
or semiconscious state.

Coué believed—and Claude Bristol echoes—
that you enter a natural hypnotic state twice
a day. It is during the few moments of deep
relaxation that you feel just before drifting off
to sleep at night and just again when coming
to wakefulness in the morning. Sleep researchers call this *hypnagogia*. During hypnagogia
you experience very deep bodily relaxation

while your mind floats in a non-logical, free-associative state where things seem surreal, and you may experience dream imagery or even hallucinations. But you retain control over your attention. Because of this, you have the ability to introduce suggestions to yourself. During that period Coué prescribed using his signature mantra, "Day by day, in every way, I am getting better and better." Coué taught that you should gently whisper this twenty times just before drifting off and again just as you are coming to.

You can also devise your own affirmations. Make them simple and gentle. Whisper suggestions to yourself of who you want to be and what you wish to attain. This is a uniquely valuable period of time because even though your attention is operative your rational defenses are down, and hence you are more likely to accept self-suggestion.

One theory goes that your mind can be reprogrammed like a homing device, such as a heat-seeking missile. Let's say you repeat gently to yourself, "Day by day I am coming into greater wealth." That can serve to program your subconscious mind, in effect, to make connections, to seek out relationships, to summon the self-possession that will allow you to move in a gradual, orderly fashion in the direction of the thing that you're looking for.

The hypnagogic state can work for us and also against us—and for the same reasons. Sometimes we may wake up in the pre-dawn hours, sometimes we may slip in and out of sleep, and worry with exaggerated severity about something that's going to happen at work. We then get to work or school and almost invariably find that the dragon we feared shrinks into a mouse. This experience is not uncommon for people suffering from anxiety. The fact is, when we're in the hypnagogic state we're very emotionally vulnerable. Our sense of analysis, proportion, and logic is lowered. But if you use hypnagogia *productively* you can bypass the logical faculty for good and positive reasons of reconditioning.

Coué sought to bypass the rational mind so that it would not reject new ideas or suggestions. A British Methodist minister in the mid-20th century named Leslie Weatherhead also tried to find ways of heightening the effectiveness of affirmations. Weatherhead greatly admired Coué, and he was also instrumental in recovery groups, including Alcoholics Anonymous.

Weatherhead observed that the rational or conscious mind is almost like a traffic cop. The conscious mind is supposed to direct the traffic of your thoughts, allowing in only those that are believable, measured, and realistic, and that match past experience, while screening out thoughts that seem contrary or erratic. This traffic cop does a lot of good but can also hinder you by disallowing unfamiliar positive suggestions.

Weatherhead believed that one way you could work around this problem is through continual repetition. If you doggedly attempt to "sneak past" the traffic cop you may eventually succeed. This approach proved useful for Claude when he repeatedly drew dollar signs. That image is charged with emotion. Symbols in general are very powerful. It's true of the pentagram, the crucifix, the pyramid, the obelisk, the all-seeing eye, the Star of David. All of these summon deep, primal responses. An alluring image appeals to the emotions and further helps elude the rational traffic cop of the mind.

Claude suggested placing mantras or symbols of self-suggestion everywhere: in your car, on your desk, by your bathroom mirror, even on your pillow. Place these things constantly before your eyes.

Claude talks about another self-suggestive method called the mirror technique. He prescribes using affirmations while you gaze into your own eyes in front of a mirror.

Claude tells the story of a businessman who convened a party in a hotel suite and there was a lot of liquor flowing. This businessman was drinking too quickly, and he needed to deliver a sales presentation to the party. Claude noticed the businessman slip off into a bedroom where he surreptitiously spotted him standing in front of a mirror saying, "You can do this. Now straighten up. You're sober, you're capable, you're going to go out there and deliver a great talk." He said that the man exited the room a little ruddy, a little sweaty, but he had a greater sense of self-possession and he delivered an effective talk.

Claude endorses making this mirror talking a steady practice, either daily or at moments of crisis. Why should the mirror technique work? It could be that there's a kind of self-hypnosis occurring. We are focused on our own reflected image so we may be liberated from some of the conditioning and rational pushback that we otherwise experience. Interrupting your rote internal or repetitive thoughts can also be a powerful hypnotic technique. Focusing on your mirror image may help do that. Hence, a mild hypnotic effect may be at work when gazing into a mirror and speaking to yourself.

It could also be, as I was referencing earlier, that Claude is correct about thought possessing a psychokinetic or vibratory frequency; and if you can focus that frequency, so to speak, you may be able to affect the firing of neural pathways in your brain. You may be enacting a kind of instantaneous neuroplasticity, perhaps by some sort of kinetic ability. (Neuroplasticity is when sustained thoughts alter the pattern of electrical impulses in your brain.) I mentioned earlier that J.B. Rhine, the pioneering psychical researcher, had done experiments for psychokinesis with throws of dice and he got results.

Years later, a group of psychical researchers at Princeton University performed long-running experiments with a technology called random number generators. The Princeton researchers found that if subjects focused on the patterns of a random number generator, which emits entirely random numerical chains (this is the same technology used to produce computer passwords), signals would sometimes appear in the noise. Certain patterns or repetitions would emerge. It could be that these extrasensory capacities, which Claude identified on a more metaphorical scale, can alter subtle electrical signals within our neural pathways. This is highly speculative but not outside of what has been observed in neuroplasticity.

It is likely that focusing on yourself when gazing in a mirror could also produce a kind of hypnagogic effect. As mentioned, hypnagogia is prime time for self-suggestion. It's also prime time for the appearance of ESP or psychical-related phenomena. In the 1970s and 80s, a brilliant psychical researcher named Charles Honorton (1946–1992) performed a series of ESP trials called the ganzfeld experiments. Very simply, the ganzfeld experiments involved placing a subject into a state of relaxed sensory deprivation, often inside of an isolation chamber, which was usually a comfortable, noise-proof room. The subject might sit in a recliner fitted with white-noise headphones and eyeshades. This comfortable state of sensory deprivation induces hypnagogia. Honorton and his colleagues discovered that when placed in such a state subjects demonstrated higher capacities for ESP-related activity.

Like Rhine's work, these experiments were conducted across many thousands of trials. They were heavily scrutinized by skeptics. In fact, Charles Honorton collaborated with a skeptic, a psychologist at the University of Oregon named Ray Hyman. The two coauthored a paper in which Hyman noted that he did not accept the ESP thesis but he affirmed that the data was unpolluted and that some of transfer of information was being registered; he agreed that it warranted further research.

That was one of the rare moments where a principled skeptic actually reviewed and familiarized himself with data coming out of serious psychical research and concluded that the data was sound. The two men had different interpretations of the implications but their collaboration was productive. Unfortunately, Honorton died at too young an age for this joint work to continue.

My point is that different possibilities emerge from this highly suggestive state of hypnagogia. It is possible that this state and the corresponding effects occur whenever you are deeply relaxed, diverted from normal sensory disruption, but also mentally aware and active. This state could occur when gazing in a mirror, entering a trance, or listening to ASMR recordings.

At such times, you may succeed not only in issuing self-suggestions, but in issuing suggestions to others, as well. Honorton's experiments focused specifically on telepathy. On a personal scale, these are highly unstructured but potentially powerful experiments to attempt. Try them and stick with them. These exercises require little effort and the results can be extraordinary.

# CHAPTER FIVE

# The Magic of the Written Word

In this final lesson, we will explore how to write down your desires as a method toward enacting them.

Claude Bristol was a great believer in the power of the written word. Claude repeatedly pointed out, as I've alluded, that signs, symbols, and phrases can serve as personal talismans, reminding you of what you want, focusing your desires and passions, always keeping your mind steady and directed, so that you are a kind of transmitting station that is ever operative, ever active in the direction of your desires.

I believe very strongly in the power of writing down affirmations, desires, and aims. And I mean writing these things down tactilely not on a device or a tablet. The act of writing with pencil or pen on paper is a first step, however small, toward the actualization of what you want to realize. It is a nascent act of creation.

I want to review three different ways that you can write down desires as a path towards their actualization. The first is a method that I resisted for a long time but eventually came around to. That is writing down a sum of money and the date by which you wish to receive it, even if incrementally, and the tasks that you're going to perform in exchange for this money.

I resisted this because I felt that writing down a sum and a deadline seemed excessively materialist or potentially limiting. Some tendency in me ran counter to naming a dollar amount. I eventually dropped my reservations almost as a matter of experiment. With the encouragement from Napoleon Hill's wonderful book *Think and Grow Rich* I decided that I would try this step.

While I was reading *Think and Grow Rich*, I decided to write down a very definite sum, a bold sum, though not outrageous, and the date by which I wanted to receive it. I wrote a date that was about a year hence and happened to be my birthday, which is November 23rd. I also wrote down what I intended to do to receive this sum. I was very interested in stepping up my narration and recording of audio books. I was also writing at an increasingly prodigious and thorough pace. These were the tasks that I wanted to deliver in exchange for this sum of money.

Oddly enough, I wrote this down on a yellow sticky note, tucked it inside the copy of *Think and Grow Rich*—I own several—and forgot about it. I returned to that particular copy of the book many months later having not even recalled writing this note. I discovered to my delight and surprise that I *had* received something very close to that sum and by the deadline designated.

It seems to me that writing down that sum, although I may have consciously forgotten the act, did create a touchstone, a beacon, so to speak, within my subconscious, and I think it helped me focus on where I was going, what I wanted, and it may have heightened potentials, both physical and extra-physical, that we have been exploring.

Seekers have a strange relationship with money. We often feel that we want more of it, but we think it's gauche or selfish or unspiritual to name an amount. Yet, I think that asking for something you want is crucially important. Many of us are undervalued. Many of us don't ask enough for the productive tasks that we do. I think it is important to be frank with yourself, to set goals, dates, and deadlines, and to also be certain that you're delivering something of concretely productive value in exchange for the sum you write down.

Having a productive goal to which you attach a dollar amount is not the same thing as cornering people to read your novel or your screenplay. You must produce something that is unambiguously part of a circuit of value that brings benefit to others. If, by the way, that happens to be your novel or your screenplay, then bravo. What I'm saying is, we sometimes spend too much time imposing on others and thinking that we're providing value. I want your sum of money and its deadline to be fixed to a very concrete, productive thing that's going to solve a problem. That to me, is the goal to which you can appropriately attach a sum.

Let me offer another written exercise, which I call the three-step miracle. It is inspired by the work of a Chicago sales executive named Roy Herbert Jarrett (1874–1937), who I admire greatly and who I write about in my book *One Simple Idea*. Roy codified his program into a 28-page pamphlet that he wrote in 1926, called *It Works*. Roy had spent his entire life studying the workings of mind metaphysics. And like Claude Bristol, he didn't actually write anything until he was well into middle age. When Roy was about 52, he wrote this little pamphlet, believing that he had come up with a formula that harnesses the very best in mind metaphysics, and I want to share my version of it with you.

It really comes down to three very basic, very simple steps. They're so simple that most serious people will neglect them. Many people will feel that they're too simple to be believed. But I have worked with this exercise for many years and I can personally validate its effectiveness.

Step one, write down, again, using pencil and paper, a list of the things that you really want in life. Refine this list, get it just right, and spend days or even weeks doing so if you feel the need.

The point of this list is to be completely self-disclosing and honest about what you want. It's a private exercise, as are the others that I've been describing, so you do not need to—and I urge you not to—seek the approval or approbation of others. I want you to feel fully free and without inhibition. The truth must be accompanied by a brave absence of embarrassment. There's no one to convince. There's no one to seek peer approval from. This is your exquisitely private exercise. It should fill you with a sense of joy. This is your opportunity to disclose to no one but yourself exactly what you want.

Once you feel you have your list well formulated—it doesn't have to be perfect and there can be changes and additions later—but once you feel it's in a place of integrity you move on to step two. This involves transferring your list to a notecard or a pocket pad or something that you can carry around with you. Produce an integral finished version of your list and carry it with you everywhere. Think about it all the time. Read your list *at least three times a day* in the morning, just as you're getting out of bed, at midday when you might be taking a lunch break, and in the evening just before you lay down to go to sleep. Make the list a constant companion. Dwell on it. Think of it always.

Third and finally, *remain silent*. Disclose what you're doing to no one. Simply express gratitude each time items on that list come to you. And they will come to you. I feel very convinced of that based on personal experience. Why? Why should writing down your desires, carrying around the list, reviewing it, remaining silent, and expressing thanks amount to anything at all?

Well, for one thing, I firmly believe, as I've alluded at other points, that we are not honest with ourselves; that we are deeply inhibited in terms of acknowledging internally what we really want. We think we know what we want. But the act of making a special effort to be truly transparent can net surprising results. Clarification can move us, consciously and otherwise, in surprising directions.

I do believe there is an ESP of daily life. It may be inconsistent, but it is there. I do believe that we are conveying our attitudes, wants, and needs to other people in extrasensory ways, even if intermittently. When you encounter somebody who's sympathetic, who may be capable of meeting you halfway or lending a hand, I think those faculties may be at play. They are also at play when people bully us, which suggests the importance of having a positive self-image and a clear sense of boundaries. Those traits, in the positive or negative, are communicated too.

As explored earlier, I believe that we may be constantly and at all times selecting different outcomes, actualities, and episodes of past, present, future from the infinitude of events and occurrences within which we live; we make these selections through our perspective, assumptions, mental pictures, and emotionalized thoughts. Do you begin to see why I place so much emphasis on honest, unadorned clarity? The stakes may be higher than we believe.

Finally, I always say that a goal, in order to be a real goal, should be actionable in some way. You should be able to take concrete steps toward it, however small. Otherwise, it's escapism. The act of writing something down is an opening step, which begins the selection process.

You may have a short-term goal that's very important to you. I've spoken about waiting periods, gestation, and different channels of delivery. All of that is very important. But I now want to provide you with a very special writing exercise that can satisfy an urgent, short-term need.

This came to me one day when I was in Boulder, Colorado, shooting a television show. I woke up one morning, feeling very depressed. There was bad weather outside and for a variety of reasons my energy was very low.

At that moment, I received an email from a reader who told me that she had been struggling for a long time with a path of mind metaphysics. She felt there was truth there. She felt there was possibility there. But she wasn't experiencing progress. Since I was in a low state myself, I decided to come up with an exercise that my unknown correspondent and I could do together. We didn't have to disclose what we were doing to one another but sometimes there is special energy in doing a joint exercise, even if you have different goals.

I devised what I call the 10-Day Miracle Challenge. It is very simple but powerful. For this particular exercise, you select one thing that you deeply need in the near-term. It can be anything. Once you feel you have a heartfelt wish over which you experience no internal compromise or contradiction, write it down.

After you've done that, create a simple grid of ten boxes. Each evening cross out one of the boxes. During each of the ten days, use every method and exercise that we have covered in this lesson plan to focus on your one immediately felt, meaningful desire. You can add other exercises as well. Pray, affirm, and visualize just before you go to sleep at night, just as you're waking up in the morning. Do everything you can to healthfully focus on that wish over this period of ten days. No method is superfluous or verboten—do everything that feels natural.

During this process and immediately after, watch *very carefully* for the arrival of what you need. Again the channel of delivery may seem routine, so much so that you may overlook the wished-for thing or condition when it comes. Or the channel can be unexpected, so that arrival may radically differ from your mind's eye picture of your fulfillment. Reject nothing.

We form limiting habits of expectancy. This exercise is useful because it helps break up those habits.

I think there's too much resistance to certain possibilities within our alternative spiritual culture. For example—and to some people this is heterodox—the thing you're looking for may reach you in the form of a pill. Mainstream medicine and pharmacology are perfectly fine things to avail yourself of, as are alternative modalities. That's what I mean when I say something could reach you along unexpected lines.

There's an old joke I grew up with. A minister climbed to the top of his church to escape a flood and prayed to God to be rescued. A rowboat came along and the rowers said, "Minister, hop on." He said, "No, God will save me." Then a raft came along and someone said, "Minister, come aboard." He said, "No, God will save me." As the waters continued to rise, a helicopter flew overhead, dropped down a ladder, and the pilot yelled, "Minister climb up." He said, "No, God will save me." Eventually the waters engulfed him and he drowned. When he got to heaven, he confronted God and said, "All my life I've served you. Why didn't you save me?" God replied, "What do you mean I didn't save you? I sent the rowboat. I sent the raft. I sent the helicopter . . ."

Life can be that way sometimes. We get thrown lifelines but we don't recognize them. Extraordinary things occur, but they don't always reach you through extraordinary channels. That is why you must be watchful and unprejudiced.

In my personal experience, this exercise works. I would never prescribe something that I hadn't personally used and found success with. I have shared this exercise with a broad range of people, including business owners, artists, physicians, and many have returned to me with remarkable testimonials. (I reprint some of these in my book *The Miracle Habits*.) I think there's something powerful in challenging ourselves. In throwing down a gauntlet and saying, "Look, ten days is enough time for something to happen in my world." It's also a sufficiently limited amount of time so that you do not lose mental focus.

During your ten days, do not get stymied by orthodoxy. I believe strongly in mixing and matching all kinds of different methods. I also believe *there's no wrong way to affirm. There's no wrong way to pray. There's no wrong way to visualize.* In the alternative spiritual culture, we get too hung up on the question of whether an affirmation should be written in future tense or present tense. Some people say that if you write your affirmation in future tense, it's as if you're pushing it off to some unforeseen point and you'll be perpetually in a state of unfulfilled expectancy. I don't think that's correct.

I don't think it matters much whether you affirm and write in present or future tense, whether you pray feeling that you've already received or whether you pray as a demand or if you implore whatever your conception of a higher power. The important thing is that what you write down, what you affirm, what you utter in prayer, be *emotionally persuasive* to you. Don't get hung up on the rules; because there are no rules.

Truth has no fences. The one important thing is to recognize yourself as a creative being. Whatever circumstances are facing you, you are never wholly without devices. You are never without possibilities. Although we experience many laws and forces, the mind is a tool that we make insufficient use of. The emotively focused and deliberate mind—what some call positive thinking—enlists energies that exceed cognition and motor functioning. This power is your birthright. That's why I believe there's no "wrong way" to approach this material.

I've often asked myself, why is *The Magic of Believing* so enduringly popular? There are lots of good books on mind metaphysics. There are beloved authors from Ernest Holmes to Joseph Murphy to Florence Scovel Shinn, and many more.

Claude Bristol is not one of the best-known authors in the field (though this is changing). As I mentioned earlier, Claude produced just two books. One of them, *TNT*, was a pamphlet. He wrote *The Magic of Believing* in 1948, just three years before his death. Yet, even in the absence of its author, the book took flight. I think the reason is that Claude knew how to meet people where they live. He echoed back to them the sense of their own larger potential without asking them to compromise their workaday needs. Claude understood that our needs involve creative expression, romance, money, health, and success—he asked no one to apologize for that.

I don't want you or anyone to feel embarrassed about wishing for any of these things. Sometimes people come to me and say they feel shy or timid about expressing their wishes, because they feel like the thing toward which they're working seems materialistic or conventional. My contention is that all the things I've just mentioned are basics of life. We express so much of ourselves through those outlets.

Claude also possessed a metaphysical vision, a vision of the mind as possessing and evincing extra-physical powers, and although he sometimes referenced prayer or God he asked no one to subscribe to any particular perspective on the spiritual. To me, spirituality is quite simply a search for the extra-physical. I think Claude saw it that way, as well.

Claude asked you to identify a higher power as *you understand it*, not *as he understood it*. He honored his reader enough to offer him or her a metaphysical vision without insisting upon fixed forms, language, or doctrine. Claude identified in *The Magic of Believing* the metaphysics of daily life—and they're yours to use.

# AFTERWORD

# Claude M. Bristol and the Metaphysics of Success*

The American metaphysical scene has produced no other figure quite like Claude M. Bristol. Born in 1891, in Portland, Oregon, Bristol had a background as varied as the nation itself: a veteran, a spiritual seeker, a sometime journalist, a sometime businessman, and an enthusiast of the possibilities and powers of the mind.

---

* This article originally appeared at HarvBishop.com in 2016.

In 1948, Bristol's personal interests in metaphysics led him, at age 57, just three years before his death, to write his enduring New Thought classic *The Magic of Believing.*

The impetus for the book began earlier in Bristol's life. As a World War I veteran, he came home to a nation in transition. The American economy was growing and the mass of young men returning from the war, many of whom came from agrarian roots and had never worked in manufacturing or in large offices, were unsure how to enter the new economy. Bristol believed that the threshold of prosperity began in the mind. He spread his theories and wrote his two and only books—the first *TNT: It Rocks the Earth* in 1932—to expose veterans and others to his ideas about the causative properties of thought.

In *The Magic of Believing*, Bristol's more developed book, self-help readers encountered topics that are rarely held in high repute today: ESP, telepathy, and psychokinesis, among them. When I recently abridged and narrated *The Magic of Believing,* I made the decision to retain this material—and I did not do so lightly. As I've written in *One Simple Idea,* my own analysis of the positive-thinking movement, I believe that many journalists and academics today have failed to understand, or even attain basic familiarity with, the experiments to which Bristol refers, particularly those conducted by ESP researcher J.B. Rhine at Duke University beginning in the early 1930s.

I take seriously Bristol's contention that legitimate parapsychology has something to offer the motivational reader. Speaking as a personal seeker and historian who has considered this field, I can vouch for the general validity of Bristol's popularizations and suggested applications of some of Rhine's parapsychological experiments. Indeed, Bristol was one of the few positive-mind theorists of his day who rightly highlighted the work of Rhine and his contemporaries.

Bristol, in his way, made large questions about the mind seem simple—because he believed that meaningful personal experiments *were* possible, and could demonstrate, or at least suggest, the efficacy of positive-mind mechanics in daily life, including in matters of career, creativity, and relationships.

Many readers swore by *The Magic of Believing*, including entertainers Liberace and Phyllis Diller. Liberace wrote a foreword to one of Bristol's editions, published in 1955 as a "Special Liberace Edition." In 1956 the piano maestro released a tributary song, "The Magic of Believing."

The famously brash Diller said that Bristol's book helped her overcome crippling shyness (a claim I have no immediate problem believing). The comedienne spoke ingenuously about her experience in interviews. Scientific authorities might be unimpressed with such testimony, but it does give a sense of the depth of dedication that Bristol's work inspired. *The Magic of Believing* was such a post-war favorite that it was even adapted into a young readers' version in 1957.

The young readers' adaption failed to catch on, however. At more than 200 pages, it was almost the length of the original, and no simpler. But it is the kind of publishing endeavor that I would like to see more of today. Despite the enduring popularity of New Thought books, few editions are available for children and teens.

Although Bristol sometimes uses dated language and a credulous tone, *The Magic of Believing* remains a surprising and radical journey into the possibilities of the mind. We are still at the early stages of grappling with some of his topics, gaining a glimpse of anomalous mental capacities in a new wave of experiments in placebo studies, neuroplasticity, precognition, and quantum theorizing.

I suggest approaching *The Magic of Believing* in a spirit of enthusiasm and personal adventure. It's an old favorite that may reignite the sense excitement you felt when first discovering New Thought.

# About the Author

**Mitch Horowitz** is a historian of alternative spirituality and one of today's most literate voices of esoterica, mysticism, and the occult.

Mitch illuminates outsider history, explains its relevance to contemporary life, and reveals the longstanding quest to bring empowerment and agency to the human condition.

He is widely credited with returning the term "New Age" to respectable use and is among the few occult writers whose work touches the bases of academic scholarship, national journalism, and subculture cred.

Mitch is a 2020 writer-in-residence at the New York Public Library, lecturer-in-residence at the Philosophical Research Society in Los Angeles, and the PEN Award-winning author of books including *Occult America; One Simple*

*Idea: How Positive Thinking Reshaped Modern Life*; and *The Miracle Club.*

He has discussed alternative spirituality on CBS Sunday Morning, Dateline NBC, Vox/Netflix's *Explained*, and AMC Shudder's *Cursed Films*, an official selection of SXSW 2020. Mitch is collaborating with director Ronni Thomas (Tribeca Film Festival) on a feature documentary about the occult classic *The Kybalion*, shot on location in Egypt and releasing in summer 2020.

Mitch has written on everything from the war on witches to the secret life of Ronald Reagan for *The New York Times, The Wall Street Journal, The Washington Post, Time, Politico*, and a wide range of 'zines and scholarly journals. He narrates audio books including *Alcoholics Anonymous* and *Raven: The Untold Story of the Rev. Jim Jones and His People* (the author of which handpicked him as the voice of Jones).

Mitch's book *Awakened Mind* is one of the first works of New Thought translated and published in Arabic.

Mitch received the 2019 Walden Award for Interfaith/Intercultural Understanding. The Chinese government has censored his work.

Twitter: @MitchHorowitz | Instagram: @Mitch Horowitz23 | www.MitchHorowitz.com

9 781722 502324